MY FAVORITE DOG

BOXERS

by Beth Adelman, MS
Former editor, *American Kennel Club Gazette*

Kaleidoscope
Minneapolis, MN

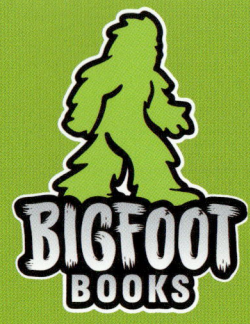

The Quest for Discovery Never Ends

·······································

This edition first published in 2021 by Kaleidoscope Publishing, Inc.

No part of this publication may be reproduced in whole or in part without written permission of the publisher.

For information regarding permission, write to Kaleidoscope Publishing, Inc. 6012 Blue Circle Drive Minnetonka, MN 55343

Library of Congress Control Number 2020936271

ISBN 978-1-64519-460-6 (library bound) 978-1-64519-462-0 (ebook)

Text copyright © 2021 by Kaleidoscope Publishing, Inc. All-Star Sports, Bigfoot Books, and associated logos are trademarks and/or registered trademarks of Kaleidoscope Publishing, Inc.

Printed in the United States of America.

Bigfoot lurks within one of the images in this book. It's up to you to find him!

TABLE OF CONTENTS

Introduction 4

Chapter 1: The Story of Boxers 6

Chapter 2: Looking at a Boxer 12

Chapter 3: Meet a Boxer! 18

Chapter 4: Caring for a Boxer 22

Beyond the Book *28*
Research Ninja *29*
Further Resources *30*
Glossary *31*
Index *32*
Photo Credits *32*
About the Author *32*

Introduction
Here Comes a Boxer!

For as long as Kei could remember, his grandfather had Boxers. Grandpa loved Boxers. Sometimes he had one, and sometimes he had two. Kei always liked to visit Grandpa. Then he could play with the Boxers.

Grandpa lived in a big house with a big backyard. He had plenty of room to keep his Boxers. But one day, Grandpa decided on a change. He wanted to move to a small apartment. It was not a good place to keep a Boxer.

Grandpa called Kei's parents. Would they like to adopt his Boxer, Akio?

"What do you think?" Kei's dad asked. "Should we take Akio?"

"Yes, yes, *pleaaaase*!" Kei was so happy. He really loved Akio. Now the big dog would be his!

FUN FACT

Boxers are distantly related to Bulldogs and Mastiffs.

Chapter 1
The Story of Boxers

Boxers have very ancient **ancestors**: the war dogs of the Assyrian Empire. They lived more than four thousand years ago. Over time, these dogs became a breed called the Bullenbeisser. They were hunting dogs for big animals like wild boar and bears. In the past, that breed was found all over Europe.

NAME TIME

Nobody is really sure where the name Boxer came from. In Belgium, the dogs were sometimes called Boxl. In Bavaria, a part of Germany, they were called Boxerl. The name probably came from those words.

Bullenbeissers are no longer around today. But some dogs in Belgium were bred with smaller dogs. The new breeds included the Boxer.

The breed we see today was developed in Germany in the late 1800s. Those dogs all had jobs. They worked with butchers and police officers and soldiers.

The first Boxers came to the United States in 1904. But they did not really become common as pets in America.

During World War II, they were used a lot by the armies on both sides. They worked as guard dogs and **messengers**. The war ended in 1945. American soldiers brought home Boxers from Germany. People saw that Boxers made great family dogs. They started to become popular.

DOGS OF WAR

The very first dog to become a Marine was a Boxer named Fritz. He joined in 1943 at the War Dog Training Center in North Carolina. Fritz's trainer described him as a "very tractable dog and excellent worker."

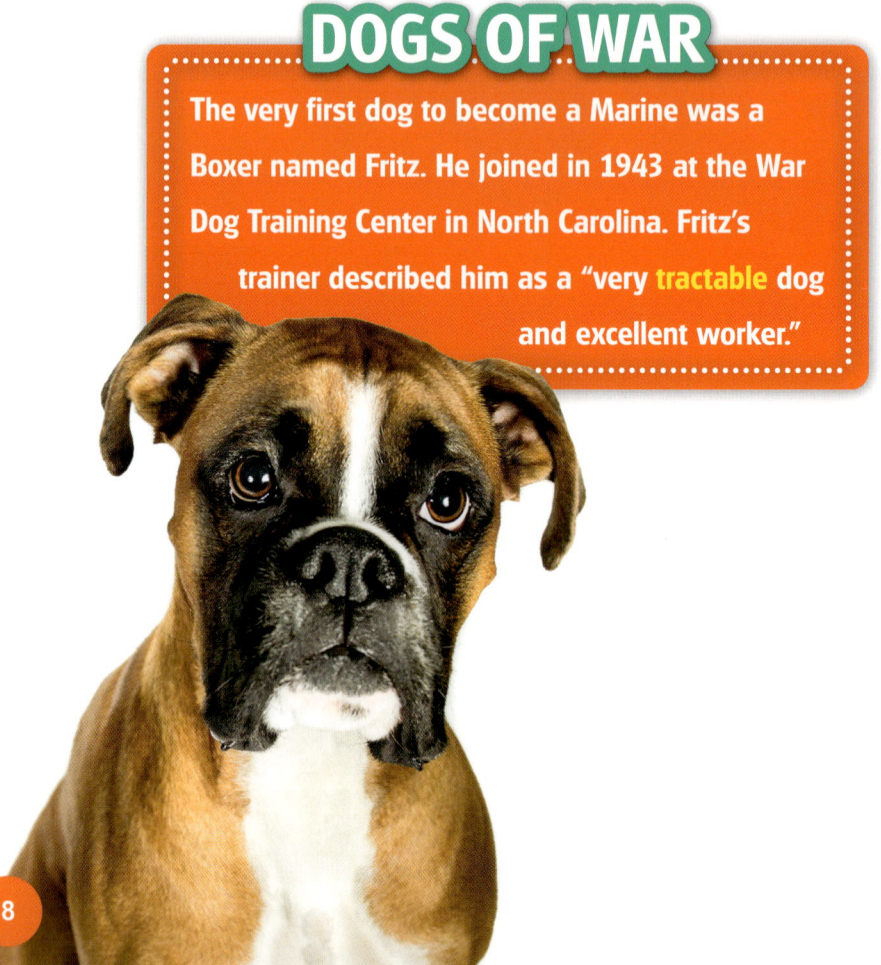

At dog shows, Boxers follow in the footsteps of Bang Away.

In 1951, a Boxer named Bang Away won the top prize at the famous Westminster Kennel Club Dog Show. It was one of 121 dog shows Bang Away won in his lifetime! The powerful, stylish dog became a huge celebrity. He was so famous that stories were written about him in magazines. He flew to dog shows as a regular passenger in airplanes. When he died in 1957, it was reported in all the newspapers. Bang Away helped Boxers become one of America's most popular breeds.

The ancestors of Boxers were fierce dogs. Boxers today are famous for being great family dogs. They love their people and just want to be with them. Kei has grown up around Grandpa's Boxers, and they have always been sweet and gentle with him.

But Boxers are not the right type of dog for everyone. They are big and need a lot of space. Big dogs always need to be trained. Otherwise they may accidentally knock over things—and people. Boxers need a lot of time and attention, too. They are not happy spending all day alone.

FUN FACT

Justin Timberlake, Jennifer Love Hewitt, Gisele Bundchen, and Ryan Reynolds are among the many celebrities who have Boxers.

Chapter 2
Looking at a Boxer

A lot of people think the most beautiful part of a Boxer is his head. Kei thinks it looks like it was carved out of stone. Akio has a strong, curved neck, too.

Boxers have short **muzzles**. Their faces have some wrinkles. When Akio is thinking about

WHAT A LICKER!

A Boxer named Brandy holds the Guinness World Record for the longest dog tongue. Brandy's tongue was 17 inches (43 cm) long. That's 2 inches (5 cm) more than a bowling pin! Brandy lived in St. Clair Shores, Michigan, and died in 2002.

something, the wrinkles on his forehead move. Kei thinks this makes him look very smart.

Boxers look like athletes. They are powerful, graceful dogs. Their long legs look thin, but they are very powerful. Boxers also have thick chests.

Kei thinks Akio looks like a superhero dog.

THE BOXER

POSTURE
Standing, spine slopes from front to back

TAIL
Carried up, whether it is long or short

MALES
HEIGHT*:
23–25 in. (58–63 cm)

WEIGHT:
65–80 lbs. (29–36 kg)

FEMALES
HEIGHT*:
21.5–23.5 in. (55–60 cm)

WEIGHT:
50–65 lbs. (23–29 kg)

*The height of a dog is measured from the top of the shoulder, not from the top of the head.

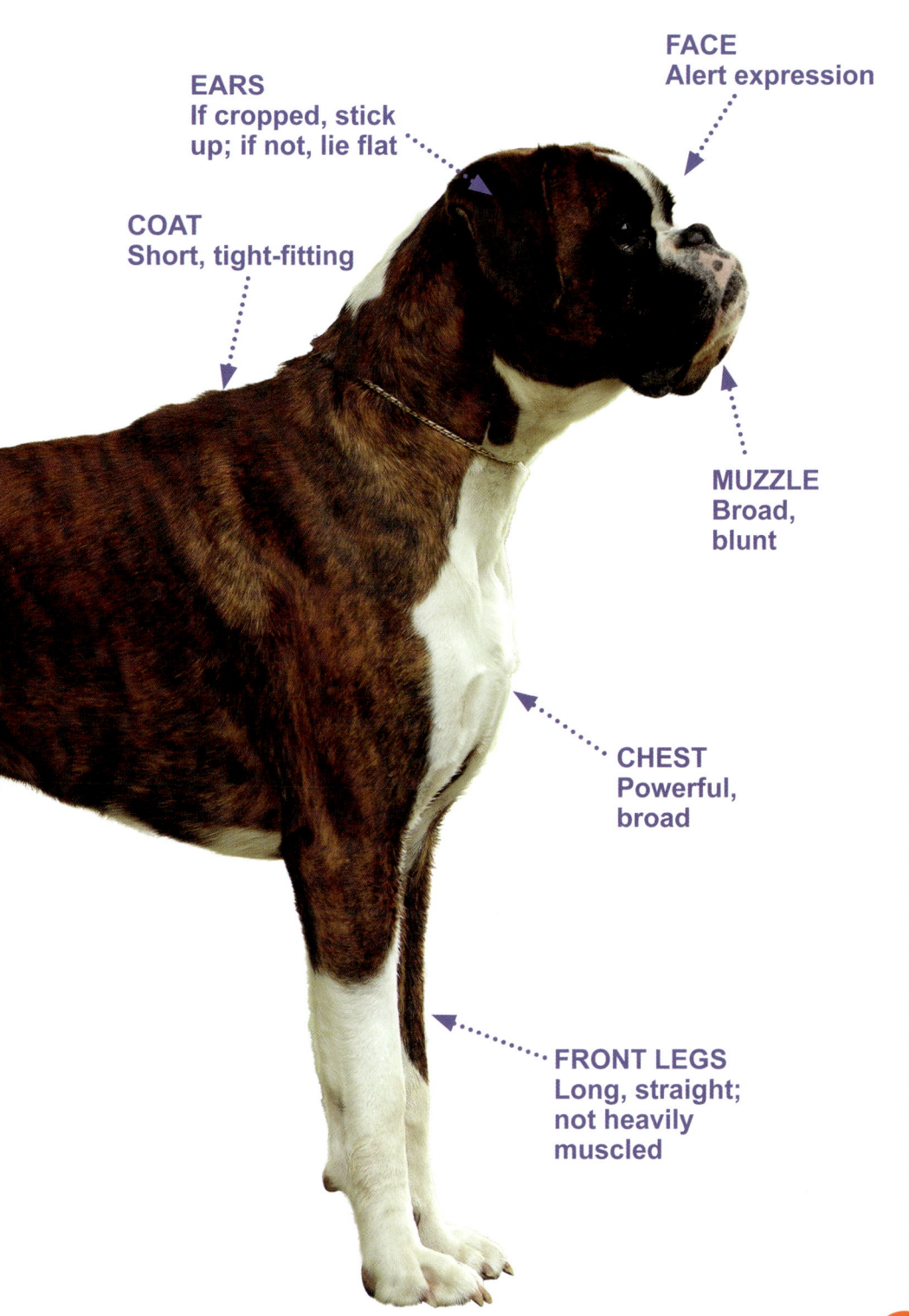

Akio's ears are soft and hang down. Some people like to cut off part of a Boxer's ears so they stand up all the way. These are called **cropped ears**. They think this makes the dog look more fierce. The first Boxers in Germany had their ears cut like this. But in Japan, where Grandpa is from, people love their Boxers just the way they are. They never cut their ears to change their looks.

Kei loves the way Akio's ears show what he is feeling. When he is excited or happy, they come forward on his forehead.

Boxers have short, shiny coats. You can see all their muscles underneath. The coat could be fawn—a color that ranges from tan to reddish brown. It could also be brindle. That's a pattern of dark brown or black stripes on a brown or red background. Many Boxers have white patches in their coats, too.

FUN FACT
All-white Boxers can't be shown at dog shows. But they can still make great pets.

Chapter 3
Meet a Boxer!

Boxers are super smart. They do well in all kinds of dog sports. Because they love people so much, they can also work as service dogs. These are dogs who help people with everyday tasks. Boxers are often used as guide dogs for the blind, and help people in other ways, too.

Because they are so smart, Boxers can get bored doing the same old thing every day. Kei spends a lot of time inventing new games to play with Akio. Just throwing a tennis ball for him would quickly become too boring.

Boxers are famous for doing a little dance when they get excited. They curve and twist their bodies. Then they start turning in circles!

Akio is really funny. He likes to act goofy. He sometimes grabs a sneaker and runs away with it. He sometimes rolls around on the ground just to make Kei laugh. Sometimes, he even bows down, sticks his rear end in the air, and wiggles his butt.

When Boxers greet the people they love, they can get very excited. They might jump up and down a lot. Because they are big and powerful, they might knock someone over. That's why Grandpa started training Akio when he was just a puppy.

Akio knows how to sit when he greets a person. He knows how to walk on a leash without pulling. He knows a lot of tricks, too.

Grandpa used to let Kei help him train his Boxers. Kei learned that the best way to train a dog is with rewards. When he does the right thing, the dog gets something he likes. It might be a treat. It might be a game. It might be Kei saying, "Good boy, Akio!" What if Akio does something wrong? Kei just asks him to do a different thing. Then Akio gets a reward!

A BIT MESSY

Some Boxers drool a lot. Owners can help by brushing their Boxers' teeth often. The dogs drool a lot after eating. Have some clean towels or wipes handy at meal times. Also, because of their short muzzles, some Boxers snore!

Chapter 4
Caring for a Boxer

Sometimes Akio gets dirty playing outside with Kei. When they come home, Kei rubs him with a towel to get the dirt off Akio's coat.

Once a week, Kei brushes Akio's beautiful brindle and white coat. He uses a curry brush. That's a soft rubber brush with little nubs on it. The brush takes out dirt and dead hair. Then Akio's coat shines.

Because of their short muzzles, Boxers don't do well in hot weather. Because of their short coats, they don't do well in cold weather, either. They should stay in the house when it's chilly, or only go out to play for a short time.

Kei uses a soft cloth to wipe the underside of Akio's ears. He cleans inside the ears with a cotton ball. But he never sticks anything in Akio's ears!

To finish the **grooming** job, Kei uses a big cotton ball to wipe between the wrinkles on Akio's face. He makes sure everything stays clean and dry.

Akio eats breakfast and dinner every day. At breakfast he eats meaty food from a can. At dinner he eats crunchy food from a bag. Grandpa picked out healthy dog foods for Akio. The foods are full of the things Akio needs to stay strong and active. He showed Kei's family what Akio likes to eat. Now Kei makes sure Akio gets the right kind of dog food. He makes sure Akio doesn't eat too much or too little.

Every day, Kei spends time training Akio. He gets some treats as a reward. He likes his afternoon snacks!

DOGS NEED CHECK-UPS

Akio goes to the **veterinarian** twice a year. The veterinarian checks to make sure he is healthy. She weighs him to see if he is fat or skinny or just right. He also goes to the veterinarian if he is not feeling well. How can Kei tell? A sick dog might eat less. Or play less. Or sleep more. Or act grouchy.

It's almost bed time. Kei's dad takes Akio out for one last walk on his leash. The walk helps the Boxer settle down and go to sleep.

While they're gone, Grandpa calls. "How is Akio doing?" he asks.

"He's great!" Kei says. "I am taking really good care of him. I know you miss him. But I am so happy he came to live with us."

Akio used to sleep with Grandpa. Now he sleeps in Kei's room. The big dog waits by the bed. "Up, up," Kei says. He pats the bed and Akio jumps up. What a polite dog!

Akio lies down at the foot of the bed. His forehead wrinkles and his ears come up. He looks like he is smiling. Kei gives him a scratch on the top of his superhero head.

BEYOND
THE BOOK

After reading the book, it's time to think about what you learned. Try the following exercises to jumpstart your ideas.

RESEARCH

FIND OUT MORE. There is so much more to find out about Boxers. Visit the American Kennel Club's site to research Boxers. Or look for a Boxer Club in your area. You can meet other people who love your favorite breed!

CREATE

TIME FOR ART. As the text shows, Boxers have helped members of the military do their jobs. Gather up some markers and paper and see if you can design a special uniform that military Boxers might wear. What colors would you use? Is it something they would wear for special occasions? Or is it something they could wear on duty?

DISCOVER

LOTS OF BREEDS. This book is about your favorite dog breed. But there are hundreds more around the world. Visit the AKC site or those of other dog organizations. What other breeds can you discover? Which breeds are related to your favorite? What is the most interesting new breed you have discovered?

GROW

HELP OUT! Animal shelters can be great places to volunteer. Contact a shelter near you and find out if you can help. Or can your family donate food or gear to help rescue dogs? Find out why dogs end up in shelters. Is there anything you can do to help them find homes?

RESEARCH NINJA

Visit www.ninjaresearcher.com/4606 to learn how to take your research skills and book report writing to the next level!

RESEARCH

DIGITAL LITERACY TOOLS

SEARCH LIKE A PRO
Learn about how to use search engines to find useful websites.

FACT OR FAKE?
Discover how you can tell a trusted website from an untrustworthy resource.

TEXT DETECTIVE
Explore how to zero in on the information you need most.

SHOW YOUR WORK
Research responsibly—learn how to cite sources.

WRITE

GET TO THE POINT
Learn how to express your main ideas.

PLAN OF ATTACK
Learn prewriting exercises and create an outline.

DOWNLOADABLE REPORT FORMS

Further Resources

BOOKS

Marin, Vanessa Estrada. *Dog Training for Kids.* New York: Penguin Random House, 2019.

Newman, Aline Alexander, and Gary Weitzman, DVM. *How to Speak Dog.* Washington, D.C.: National Geographic, 2013.

Sundance, Kyra. *101 Dog Tricks: Kids Edition.* London: Quarry Books, 2014.

Sutter, Marcus. *Shipwreck on the High Seas: Soldier Dogs No. 7.* New York: HarperFestival, 2020.

WEBSITES

Factsurfer.com gives you a safe, fun way to find more information.

1. Go to www.factsurfer.com.
2. Enter "Boxers" into the search box and click 🔍
3. Select your book cover to see a list of related websites.

Glossary

ancestor: an animal in the past from which a modern animal developed.

cropped ears: ears that have been partly cut to make them stand up.

grooming: taking care of an animal's body.

messenger: someone who delivers messages.

muzzle: the nose and mouth of a dog.

tractable: easy to train.

veterinarian: a doctor for animals.

Index

Assyrian Empire, 6
Bang Away, 9
Bavaria, 6
Belgium, 6, 7, 11
BoxerI, 6
Brandy, 12
Bullenbeisser, 6, 7
coats, 15, 16, 22
dancing, 18
drooling, 21
eating, 21, 24
Fritz, 8
Germany, 6, 7, 8, 11, 16

grooming, 23
Japan, 16
Marines, 8
Michigan, 12
North Carolina, 8
service dogs, 18
training, 21, 24
veterinarian, 24
War Dog Training Center, 8
Westminster Kennel Club Dog Show, 9
World War II, 8

PHOTO CREDITS

The images in this book are reproduced through the courtesy of: Dreamstime: Donna Kilday 9. AP Images: Jamie Charboneau 12. iStock: Sisoje 21; Astrid Schur 23; peopleimages 24. Shutterstock: Rebecca Ashworth 4; ostphotos 6; Nathan Clifford 8; Jagodka 10; Anna Hoychuk 13, 26; Marcel Jancovic 14; Javier Correa 16; Karolsejnova 17; George Lee 18; Pixel Shot 19; Jasminko Ibrakovic 20; Vitaly Titov 22; Pixel-Shot 25; Hugo Felix 31.
Cover and page 1: Gelpi/Shutterstock. Paw prints: Maximillian Laschon/Shutterstock.

About the Author

Beth Adelman is a writer and animal behavior consultant in Brooklyn, New York. She writes about her two favorite things: animals and sports.